BETWEEN HURRICANES

JENNIFER RANE HANCOCK

Photos courtesy of John Robert Hancock
Design and layout by Harvey-Rosen

Between Hurricanes
Jennifer Rane Hancock
ISBN 978-0-9962170-3-3
Lithic Press

LITHIC PRESS
fine books for an old planet

www.lithicpress.com

In Memoriam

Nora Jane Sandlin Hancock
1947-2013

John Robert Hancock
1947-2014

Gail Brooks Gerlach
1943-2014

For Bonnie,
my sea star.

TABLE OF CONTENTS

CONSPIRACY THEORY

BETWEEN HURRICANES

This sky, too, is folding under you
And it's all over now, Baby Blue

Bob Dylan

CORIOLIS EFFECT

SANDPIPERS
       for DGB

a girlfriend loves the word *liminal*
        loves flirting
with the fluid edges of the way we
know things
knows how
to kiss a woman and
how to trace the edge of a man's
neck where it segues into shoulder

she's pale and blonde
and grew up in the boundary worlds
of Viet Nam and Thailand
        baby cobras hatching in the garden
        under her father's military boot
and she can describe the smell
of a monk's skin as it burns

but I'm telling her this thing
about sandpipers
over hot lime-infused soup
at the only Thai restaurant
in Stillwater, Oklahoma:

how they chase the edge of the Gulf
as it advances and retreats but
it's not really an edge
        I say
more of a dissolving of foam
into sand into
an impression
of land and I'm trying to say

I'm sad
we're landlocked
and that I wish the definition
between prairie and sky was less
            acute

I pick a stalk of lemongrass
from my soup
set it on the cheap china rim
avoid looking
at the strip mall parking lot

            Oklahoma heat shimmering
            the black-top
            Ford F-150s with gun racks
            and glittering Dixie flags

and my friend nods like she has
some knowledge
of sandpipers on distant Texas shores
their twig legs brittle
in all that uncertainty
chasing an edge that isn't an edge
wanting desperately
            for it to chase back

like she knows that's what I mean
but not what I mean
and that the question of

how we love
is one of retreat and advance
and of earth that turns to water
under our feet

HOW A HURRICANE FORMS
found poem

       like a ballerina born
not made
       between the earth's rotation
forward, invisible
       in the one direction
the optimism of fresh paint
       and the respective spin
       of the low-pressure core itself in the other,
tequila and sleeping pills, the lifting
vacuum of night
       the pirouetting tropical cyclone
her given name: wife
       begins when warm, moist air
       that has been drawn in
like a breath of lemon, dreams
confused with actual desire
       by the pressure center
the pull of the lungs
the kitchen of the house
       does not reach its revolving target
the targets we all miss
the exit on the freeway
our aim off
an open window, open
       but is instead curved to the right (or east)
the weaker side of the heart

in the northern hemisphere
> *and to the left (or west) in the southern*
> *hemisphere*

the two hemispheres of the heart
the equator running through
the foundation of a house
> *by the*

this
> *coriolis effect*

AFTER THE RAIN, THE EARTH SMELLS
LIKE A MOUTH
Echo to Narcissus I

I should have said
    the beauty I've seen in an orange

but you would have countered with
        geese flying the wrong way for February
            a finger on a full lip
        no hope of hope

and you wouldn't have meant any of it

nor I (there is no beauty in oranges
only questions without answers)

***

in the morning when you are distracted
and an egret moves through the lily pads
the words come to me more easily

***

you already know what Spanish moss
feels like under your cheek
I don't have to tell you

***

I should have left when I could
dragging bulbs and roots
behind me like a shadow

you might have noticed
might have said
     with intention comes pain
     the north sides of oak trunks

but I didn't and articulation now
strains through the watery
filter of the gaze

ENOUGH OF WANTING
Echo to Narcissus II

your tongue on my neck, you adjust
the rear-view mirror to admire your hair
falling over your Arkansas-red sweatshirt

you red-shirted your freshman year
cropped off your glorious hair for the coach
tanned your neck the color of Ozark dirt

* * *

we are in Austin now, Longhorn territory
and drinking Shiner, the future possible
as if I'm walking on water

but water is precious in a drought
and the fire ants build mounds against a future
that longs for its own reflection

* * *

there's a mole on your back you'll never see
it is precious to me, and ugly
and I'll protect you from the truth of it

the truth is I know you're lying
when you whisper that my jaw-line is precious
that you've never seen beauty that hurt like mine

* * *

it's enough for now to be naked by Lake Travis
hip to hip and mouth full of August denial
the blue sky so bright it stings

but when bluebonnets and Indian paint
fill the medians of Texas highways again
I'll know I've had enough of wanting

TOKENS FOR A SPELL
Echo to Narcissus III

It's only when I look around your flat
I find the things I want.

Not you, precisely, but
the poster you tore off the tile wall

in the Rome train station,
the flush in your cheeks

when the conductor shouted
something, the pecorino

crumbling later between your fingers,
the Chianti on your lips.

I want the flash of teeth you showed
the children who followed you

through the plaza in Barcelona,
following your trail of pennies like pigeons.

I want the touch of your hand
on my head,

I want you to find something for me
in your pocket.

Your notes from the café in Tangiers,
the brine in your hair from the ferry crossing,

market spices and mirrors, the couscous
recipe from the hotel, the words

the snake charmer worked on you.
Something I can actually use.

ALAMO TABLEAU
for MTF

I've seen it before, am long since over
the surprise at how small the building,
how centered it is in the city.

This I learned as a kid:
remember Goliad,
remember Travis and Bowie,

be brave in the face of certain failure.
And I wait for him outside the Burger King.
There's nothing amazing about the plaza,

the Woolworth's on the corner,
the shops sharing a city block
with the old mission.

There's nothing spiritual in our afternoon:
two friends on a business trip,
eating ice cream and shopping,

him browsing for his wife,
me for my husband.
We compare trinkets and postcards,

touch the moss-covered stone wall,
but there is nothing tender in the light
sifting down through the live oak.

Leaning against the wall I idly trace
the Spanish curve over the entrance,
and wonder how I should feel about this day

in my home state which is not
anymore. Mockingbird. Pecan. Bluebonnet.
I want to show him there's more

than the shopping bags and street signs,
something from my childhood dreams.
The hot summers, the cicadas,

how cool the river feels on your feet.
Across from me two mariachi players
sit on the curb. In their early twenties,

one is a woman and at first this is all I notice.
But then the man lights a cigarette,
the braid on his cuffs glinting,

and before he passes it to her he leans in,
like a bird lighting on a fountain,
and kisses her. This, then, I can show him:

these two in the shade of the Alamo,
the shade of the statue of Travis,
the umbrella over the snow-cone vendor.

AFTER SEEING ANNE SEXTON'S
CHECKBOOK IN A MUSEUM

They never really knew how honest
      you were when you wrote.
            The exact date, the precise, round zeroes.

This quiet, thin book
      not poems, but more
            than just ink on paper.

Each missing page telling a story:
      the dry-cleaners for your husband's shirt,
            a sweet bribe for your daughters,

groceries for your lover's breakfast.
      We all carry checkbooks,
            a small detail we share.

You left a sequence, pale gold slips of paper
      scattered behind you like New England leaves.
            Adulteress, you didn't choose to save

this book, of all things, to be read.
      They placed it next to a photograph of you
            mid-thirties, looking tired, under glass.

Mother. Daughter. Wife, pen in hand.
      Scarf around your hair, dark glasses
            hiding the signs of last night's drinks.

After the museum I stand in line
        at the store, scribble a bit of poetry
                on the back of my own checkbook.

I make a mental note to pay the electric bill,
        confess I want to touch the neck of a man
                who is not my husband,

shift a jar of olives to the crook of my elbow
        to write better. And I think of you, not
                rushing into the night, but glancing

in the rear-view mirror outside the A&P,
        re-touching your lipstick, following the lines
                of a wrinkle with your little finger.

SOUTH ON I-15

I want to look back so badly,
just one last glance at the neon and the buildings
and the palm trees lining the strip like dancers.

I want it to mean something that we can leave at all,
that we are stronger than the people heading into town
by the busloads. But it comes with us in the car,

desert sand collecting under the floormats like salt.
And a little while later, on the highway into California,
the last casino looms like a natural rock formation,

and I lie to you, tell you I have to pee.
Now, I say. *There won't be a gas station for miles.*
I have three quarters in my pocket,

and I know this is what it means to touch you
desperately each night, to wonder if it's the last time,
to see how high the bets will go.

HANGI FEAST: ROTORUA, NEW ZEALAND

I want to believe that I was once a cannibal,
    that this is something I would remember:
        I am standing nose-to-nose with a Maori man
    whose skin smells almost good enough
to eat. His pheromones, perhaps,
    or the sulfur from nearby mud pools, or the food
        in the underground pit, or even my lover
    in line behind me waiting his turn
to greet this man, curling the unfamiliar words
    we've been taught around his own tongue.

I've stepped into the space around this stranger's
    body with a southern reserve, leaned my head
        forward until my face met his and I am stunned
    by the skin of his cheek, the heat against mine,
the surprise kiss of eyelash. But he does this every
    night, coaxing tourists out of their shells
        at the Tamaki Village, yawning later against
    his wife's back. It's just a job. *Aotearoa,* he says to me.
(Land of the long, white cloud). And I think:

Yes. To the fog uncurling in the tree ferns,
    the geothermal steam sliding over my ankles.
        This is the connection we all crave,
    the absolute, the physical chemistry of touch,
the solidity, the hollows of our bodies capable
    of anything. I could inhale him, hook my leg
        behind his knees and push him into the rough,
    volcanic dirt, take that first bite at the tendon
where neck meets shoulder, follow my tongue
    along the crook of his arm, cupping his elbow

to my mouth. If this isn't quite hunger,
  it's the press of his nose against mine
      once more, and I taste the syllables he's about
  to exhale: *Kia ora*. Welcome. And then again,
waiting for me: *Kia ora*. And my mouth opens
    like a flightless bird and I reply: *Kia ora . . . sustenance.*
        His eyes widen and his breath meets mine
    around that delicious, unexpected word.

ECHO POINT, BLUE MOUNTAINS

he thinks it's exotic
to be in this place where I used to live
to hear my voice fall back

into the cadence of birds
he loves it
he says

his mouth on my belly
the eucalyptus oil heavy in the air
bluing the cool mountain morning

but it isn't my body he holds
not my hips in his hands
my legs are too long somehow

my hair much too light
and the girl I saw last night
easing off the train

at the Katoomba station
in my old school uniform
(swish of a wool skirt against tights)

her hair tucked into the neck
of a dark navy blazer
walked right past us as if she knew the way

like I never did
she belongs here in the way I don't
her echo between us a lover

we both want
I almost ran after her
would have begged her to tell me

where I'd been
since we last met
what she'd done to our hair

and how she had eased
into that body
that was no longer mine

MURMUR

his ear on my heart,
he asks about that sound:
it's a small catch in the rhythm,
a gentle backwash rushing
into a tidal pool,
a hollow scoop of stone
collecting the very edge
of a wave.

the mad swirl
of white water that calms
for a breath, the still sound
of a name whispered
after the valve has shut,
a place for him to dip his feet.
anemone, tiny sideways-
moving spider, barnacle.

WALKABOUT

It has come to this returning:
the light on the smooth bark
skin of a eucalyptus,
its whiteness like the bones of animals
trailing across the outback.
Rainbow snake swallowed me whole
and vomited me up
on the wrong side of the ocean.

I came searching for this light,
this paper-bright afternoon on this slight
hill in this upside-down place.
I came tracing the witchetty grub channels
of my own Dreaming,
marking the map of my life like termite
mounds mark the boundary of a forest.
The high thin rustle of dry leaves
called to me across the Pacific,
the memory of the narcotic blue haze
of eucalyptus oil in the air.
It is the oldest place on earth.

This very spot burned two years ago,
gum nuts snapping open like firecrackers,
galahs and spiders moving east toward water
as if they had been shown the way.

I lived here for four years and
have forgotten that I ever called it home
or knew what to do in case of snakebite.
But I did this once: white girl, American,
on a walkabout in the Ku-rin-gai bush.

The subterranean hum of insects
beneath my feet,
flocks of cockatoos in the canopy,
the kangaroo mobs beating time across cracked land
sound like a didgeridoo
and echo in the bones of my ears.
      Rhythm sticks.
A bullroarer's rush like water after a drought.

WINTERING AT MOOLTUNYA

This morning at five the wallabies thump
up the porch wondering about breakfast.
I make the coffee in the French press
with the broken handle, stoke the fire
in the potbellied stove, slice some carrots
for the animals and follow my father outside.

What do I say as he confides over a slice
of toast that the woman he left my mother for
is on the brink of leaving him?
If he were any other man I'd simply lay my hand
over his and nod in the way of women.
But I was fourteen when my mother

begged him to come back, leaned against
the front door and slid down the wall.
She leaned on me—put her head in my lap
that night and moaned until dawn.
He gives me this wound like he offers me sugar
for my coffee, and we move to the porch

with vegetables for the wallabies and seed
for the crimson rosellas who scatter and fight
like children. In a week I have gone through
five rolls of film on these birds: flash of green
under their wings, thick black tongues darting
over the seeds. A low cloud sits on the hills

lacing the gum trees; I want nothing more than to
walk out into the rainforest and leave this man
who has aged without me, to find out for himself
how empty a house is, how small and lost he can feel.
But I know these things already and can tell him
he'll need a willing ear when he remembers

how she tasted like clover honey. And one day his pride
will slip down the shower drain like a skin
and he'll imagine her legs layered with another man's.
He rubs his eyes with the wrist of the hand
holding his mug, spilling a little and not caring,
and asks me why his best just leaves her cold.

A kookaburra howls in the forest like a monkey
but I don't have an answer for him;
I never found one in all these years and can only
put my feet on the railing, stretch against the chill.
You'll need someone to talk to,
I finally tell him, *to help with the little things.*

LEAVING SYDNEY

This morning, pressing my palm against the car window,
I think: this is how I can't touch you now—hand
flat on your heart, the tips of two fingers searching

for your collarbone. I'm driving south from Sydney, edging
between the coast and jade pasture. This heavy fog
has settled in the night, washing over everything

like a baptism. The diffused dawn light pushes
through the water in the air at an angle and hits the ghost
gum trees lining the highway. Their bark blazes whiter

than paper, whiter than sheets on a bed. Drowsy,
I see a herd of kangaroos arching in and out of the cloud
that clings to the earth like a blanket. They move parallel

to the road, easily faster than the car, and I turn to say
my god, do you see that? And you're not there, not
reaching for the camera or pulling your hair back

in your ballcap. Desire this morning is a thing seen
and then unseen between eucalyptus trunks: your lips
at the corner of my eye, your hand at the base of my spine,

the silhouettes of these animals like red-brown muses
from the Dreamtime. They would have turned
toward me, leapt the road if I could have asked,

if I hadn't known that this is how I will remember
losing you, disappearing and reappearing in the fog,
the most beautiful thing I may ever see.

BONE COLLECTOR

Last week on NOVA they showed
hip replacement surgery up close, loud
and splashy. My husband hollered

to turn down the noise, but he was
in the other room, and couldn't see
the ball-shaped drill easing into the thigh,

or hear each chip ping off the clamp.
And when I told him how white
her bone was against the red sponge,

he didn't believe me. Last night I piled
books around a stack of dishes, perched
them on the edge of the kitchen table

and tried to find quotes about bones
for a friend's birthday card. I found
Count Ugolino grinding his teeth

on the skulls of his children, forever crazed
at the satisfaction. And Plath sifting
through ashes for hard sounds to chisel

her poems. I picked up a chicken bone,
scraped it clean of tendons and barbecue
sauce, pressed my thumbnail into its porous

end. This, then, was a word. My husband
walked past, reminded me not to give it
to our dogs. *Betrayal? Breath?* What word

could be too fragile for dogs' teeth
but stronger than mine? I looked up from
my books, from Sexton's lover's raw-boned

wrist, from Neruda's bones crumbling
in a foreign country, from the bones
of horses littering Cormac McCarthy's

Texas. On edge, I called my sister in Chicago—
remember the prehistoric house in the Field Museum?
Mammoth ribs arching toward the center

like a teepee? What was it I said in the doorway?
I looked at you funny, remember, and said
something. They were plaster, but

so smooth in places, like they'd been touched
repeatedly, rubbed and polished. And what
was above the doorway? It was something so terrible

we smiled, something we tried to reach.
This morning I keep feeling my cheekbones,
my elbow, the sharp point of my clavicle.

I postscript a line in my friend's card:
I know what you mean now, why you collect bones.
Something's shifted in the way I hear words.

I tell him to meet me at the junkyard
between Santa Fe and Taos,
under the billboard, where the old woman

turns piles of cattle skulls and coyote legs,
bleaching them for tourists. *It's important,
I say. I've got something to tell you.*

CAUTION: SHIFTING SAND

I lift your arm to the headboard,
trace the curve of finger into palm
and say that the way a sand dune moves
is how I will leave you. Road

disappearing into the beach, so
slowly you'll fail to notice, the fingers
of sea oats and glasswort taking
over the terrain of your life. I dig

a thumbnail mark on your shoulder,
shift the pillow to the edge of the bed,
anticipate the topography of this last
time we'll fuck, tide building ahead

of a tropical storm. The eventual receding
leaves a demarcation of debris: seaweed
coated in crude, the hulls of crustaceans,
a milk jug buoy anchored only to air.

CHILDHOOD AND ITS RATTLESNAKES

FORAY

the earth itself is fruiting and the dark longing you keep
locked until august fingers through you like fibrous

webbing. look how your relationship with truth strains
against the stronger pull of subterranean logic. see how

your posture changes, the sky becomes superfluous.
in the periphery, evidence of the usual chronology:

filling the car with gas, making toast, making love with
passion or with none. this penumbra fades into stands

of spruce and aspen, the space between greens almost
holy. you could crouch here forever, digging tenderly

at the crown of a head. russet, damp with birth, the
surface world's time slowing to the speed of a heartbeat.

LISTENING FOR BELL-BIRDS

My father cups a fungus the size
of a child's head with his hands.
He's kneeling by a strangler fig,
the fingers of roots around
the now-hollow center filtering

light like lace across his back.
We are hunting mushrooms
in the rainforest of northern
New South Wales, cameras
slung around our necks,

the Hasselblad I hope to inherit one day
around his, my Canon 35mm fitted
with a macro lens. How did we
come to this point of shutter
speed and aperture? We move

briefly into sunlight, a great hole
in the canopy where a eucalyptus fell.
He nudges the decaying bark
and carpet of leaves with his boot
and I wonder what is the equivalent

exposure of a life? We've seen
each other only three times
in ten years, but today we've drunk tea
from his thermos, consulted
his dog-eared field guide, and listened

for the sparrow-sized sirens darting
through the branches around us.
And it might be enough. I know now
how quickly he can load film.
I know he's read Barthes, and like him

loves the mechanical whir and click
of a well-made German camera.
And he's reassured himself
I'll slide down a mountain on my ass
for a shot, holding my camera high

above the mud like a good girl.
I've waited all day for him to say
good one. You nailed it, but I know
it'll take longer than we have time or light
this afternoon. He pulls a dead branch

into our patch of sun, angling the rays
onto a rust-colored fan and I wander
down the trail, hoping to hear
the elusive wind-chimes, listening
for the bellbirds, hoping I'll be so lucky.

MY PARENTS' OLD ACTING TROUPE, THE ALPHA OMEGA PLAYERS, COMES TO TOWN

Jimmy actually stood, stage left, and said
is there a doctor in the house? St. Joan is in labor.
My mother, tangled in the rough brown robe,

leaning against the wall in the middle of Scene II,
barely through the second trimester,
had missed her cue.

We are legends in this rag-tag group,
and the story grows each time it's told:
my father running lights, my mother

practicing her lines in front of the mirror.
She was so good she even knew Joan's skin,
would say later she knew what it felt like to burn.

And earlier that night, they say the whole troupe
sat in the trailer and tried to name me over spaghetti
and beer, blocked out my entrance and roughed

a script for the young parents. They were somewhere
in Pennsylvania, would hit Delaware the next night
and open *Spoon River* in a graveyard.

But all the versions end at the ambulance doors,
the house lights up in the small community theater,
the worried smiles over the pregnant Joan of Arc.

Only my mother remembers the encore,
the doctors telling her I'd kill us both,
begging her to sign a release form.

I can only imagine my father's fear,
my mother's fierce eyes,
and the way she fell back into character with a sigh.

MIDNIGHT MOVIES
for RFP

Thursdays in your '56 Ford pickup
the ghost of a lover between
us on the bench seat. You taught me

to use the column shift and not to
ride the clutch all the way into town.
Who was it that sat there, his left

thigh against yours, right hand along
my neck, cologne like burnt popcorn.
I wanted you like you wanted him

and his pouty mouth. The floorboard
boombox rocked us through the
Oklahoma prairie night: Frankenfurter

in lace and leather, sumac bleeding
at the edges of the headlights and
the cassette tape warping at the end.

The radio towers on I-35 gleamed like
drag queens lighting the way, off
to the west we see lightning

from the storms of someone else's
future, the tornado sirens silent
for the damp, hopeful moment.

FIRST KISS, PORTUGUESE MAN O' WAR

Twenty meters long and as light
as my hair on the buoyant salt water,
thin blue line like a bracelet

around my arm, heat on my thigh.
I turned into the swell, every fine hair
on my neck stiff and tingling

but saw only the Pacific, a surfer,
a gull. But when my feet found
the sand of Bondi Beach something

wrapped around me like an electrified
towel, and then pain. Fifteen
and embarrassed, an awkward imbalance

of hips and breasts, I shivered
at the lifeguard station while a man
with tawny eyes and gold hair

on his forearms poured two gallons
of chilled vinegar over my head.
It pooled at the hollow of my collarbone.

Close your eyes, he said.
Christ, didn't you see them on the beach?
I shook my head, mute and on the verge

of understanding poison
and the neurotoxins of desire. It should
have been him, I thought. His hands

cooling my skin, his fingernail tracing
the blue vein down the inside of my
arm, sand sharp against my lips.

SEPTEMBER 1976, CALM

in the lulls between hurricanes
mid-September heavy days
we waited for the Port Aransas ferry
to lock its ramp to the edge of the world

vinyl seats beach towels sticky thighs
nothing could pull the horizon down
and make the ocean boil

between hurricanes all ferries
lurched with pickups
were followed by dolphins and gulls
and all girls in terrycloth shorts
found their legs giving way
under them like on funhouse floors

between hurricanes all families
rode the continents of ferries
all captains played Van Morrison
on transistors and all fathers used
the parking breaks on '67 Chevy Novas
and held mothers who wore psychedelic
prints and chain-smoked Marlboro Lights
and sang along between hurricanes

and between hurricanes the fathers
remembered the stadium at Stephen F
the east Texas cypress dripping
with spanish moss
the way the days fell and were lost
between hot slick sex
and the first terrycloth girl baby

between hurricanes the mothers
congratulated themselves on the carefree
laughing brown-eyed girls *slippin'*
and a'slidin' the waves to port aransas

the girls swayed their terrycloth hips
between hurricanes
and held the railings and crooned
to the dolphins that all was safe
and wondered *hey where did we go,*
days when the rains came?
the dolphins followed all ferries
between hurricanes
and bobbed their noses in time
keeping time and checking
the atmospheric pressure

CHARTING HURRICANES

Delia hooked me first, a thin memory of plywood
stacked against the house, my father's mouth
full of nails from the rust-bottomed Folger's can.

Then Amelia, Claudette, and Elena, movie stars
or dancers, women with wind for hair and bodies
strong as the undertow of surf. By my birthday

in early summer the grocery bags at Kroger's
were printed with maps of the Caribbean and the Gulf,
grid-marked with longitude and latitude lines.

Bonnie and I abandoned coloring books for these,
kept a careful key of the storms we charted.
From June 1 to November 30, we crisscrossed

the ocean, giving each newly named storm a color
of her own—flamboyant disco colors or deep ocean hues
—anything that would stand out against the bag's brown.

Each night after dinner we'd meet over the radio
between our beds and listen for the coordinates.
Those letters and numbers were better than anything

Electric Company did, and we copied
them down with innocent precision.
Bonnie, too young to plot, connected the dots

I made for her, sketching improbable paths
for the storms, strange constellations linking
Ft. Lauderdale, Havana, and Brownsville.

It was usually the same male voice each night,
calling their names and positions
as if he knew their faces, as if he could bring them

right inside our bedroom and dance with them.
I thought he meant he loved them;
I thought their names said it all.

It meant women could misbehave and still
be beautiful. And after the charting, and after
checking the crab traps off the back porch

one last time for the night, she and I would sit
in the tub like two Vs nestled together,
like tight lines of isobars on a weather map.

THE NATIONAL CENTER FOR ATMOSPHERIC
RESEARCH, BOULDER, COLORADO

It was her voice that made
The sky acutest at its vanishing.
—Wallace Stevens

I.M. Pei playing with blocks as a toddler, a surety
in his choices that surprises a nearby adult.
This is easy to imagine, although perhaps untrue.

And later, his critical, dark eye scanning the Flatirons
beyond the Boulder skyline, searching for the subtle spot
where stone segued into wall-of-stone and then back

into the deepening green of juniper. Inside his building,
which I've decided is too heavy, too earth-bound
to house a bunch of meteorologists, I am reminded

that plush carpet can feel like sand between your toes.
I read a footnote behind plexiglass: *until 1979, all hurricanes*
and tropical storms were given women's names only.

And as I wander the displays, call up the archived
satellite photos of storms I thought I knew by name,
this one sentence spins my own childhood memories

counter-clockwise, demands that I finally hear
the connotations of death, the way a father names a daughter,
the way a name can become a curse to be used

as crops disappear under mudslides, or condos crumble
into the Gulf. Here, in the thin air a mile above sea-level,
I feel the shame reserved for women who never question.

If Pei were here, I'd tell him that when I was four
I wanted to be a hurricane, not a mother or a teacher.
Mom told this story to each boyfriend I ever

brought home: *She'd spin,* she'd say, conjuring
my long hair lifting away from my head like the cirrus streamers
uncurling from the edge of a storm. And she'd laugh that

mother-showing-baby-pictures-laugh and described how
finally, exhausted and dizzy, I'd slam into the avocado Formica
countertop and collapse onto the matching linoleum floor.

EVACUATION ROUTE

When Hurricane Bonnie crashed into South Carolina
last year, I called her up in Chicago and asked
why she was causing so much trouble.

Do you remember, she asked, the time we left Corpus
ahead of Amelia? The taillights stretching
over the causeway. You were so worried.

Was not, I said back. Was, too. She only remembered
the adventure, the two of us piled into the station wagon
under pillows and stuffed animals, not the last-minute

frown on Mom's face, not Dad's nod, not the lines
at the grocery store the day before, not the empty shelves.
I knew it all meant that whoever had made her way

across the ocean and slipped past the tip of the Yucatan
was bigger than the crayon dots we'd drawn,
and pissed off. That night at Uncle Allen's

in Houston, I dreamed of water swirling
past the pylons under our house, palm trees bent double
at the knees ahead of a wind so real it lifted me

from the bed. And after that dash inland, I decided
I'd learn it all. I knew the exact moment each storm
passed 74 mph sustained winds, memorized Haiti's

coordinates, and whispered *Antilles* like a chant.
The bulletins were music, like a salt breeze
through sand dollar wind chimes: *a low, vertical sheer*

in the troposphere . . . strong, mid-lateral westerly winds.
I learned to watch for the dip in the jet stream
that might mean a change of course. The Port A pier

stretched out into the water like summer, fishing twine
and lead sinkers wrapped around weathered gray posts.
We thought we could walk all the way to Florida on it.

The last time I was twelve and we were moving
inland. Bonnie was safe on the shore behind me,
building Tupperware-shaped sea walls

in the cool, wet sand. Ahead of me was the vanishing
point of the pier, a fisherman cleaning a shark carcass,
and the next storm gathering strength beyond the horizon.

STORM SURGE

to survive a direct hit
        from a storm surge
roll up your jeans
        bend like a palm
twist like a live oak

offer it nothing
        turn sideways and
make yourself thin
        avoid its notice
like the pylon houses

where you hid from your
        mother's hand her
frown in the cool
        shade mosquito
carcasses like

rhinestones on wind-
        shredded webs
and the clear blue
        Gulf between gray
pine posts echo

of a drilling platform
        on the future's
horizon pick your
        spot and hold
tight or lash yourself

like a sailor just
       ride out the surge
and subsequent
       tidal receding
 an Epsom salt bath

MOTHER MY WORRY STONE
after Dorothy Barresi

Mother my worry stone
my cautionary tale
my *pack an emergency kit*

Mother my stone in the heart

Mother my meeting place
my Book of Revelations

my hurricane warning
red flag whipping on the beach
my sand dunes dissolving

Mother my threat of leaving
Mother my lost in the East Texas swamp
one of any mothers fishing on the pier
my *pack your boxes like I told you*

Mother my garage sale
strangers picking over me

Mother my guilt my power to cut
my *how could you*
how could you

Mother my same hands
Mother my lips of stone

Mother my gather us close
my empty lungs
empty Dr. Pepper cans as ashtrays

Mother my duck-and-cover

CHILDHOOD AND ITS RATTLESNAKES

implement: your father's car key is sharp
enough to cut off the tail of the living

the living you: building lincoln log houses
for palmetto bugs crisp with promise

this crisp house: eggshells and coffee grounds
lure snakes to its pylon boundaries

the eggshell pylons: so fragile you shiver
in your sleep and the storm surge is coming

sleep: fragile in the inexplicably muggy desert
the cacti and bay bush ambivalent

the fragile rattles: lined up by the kitchen sink
proof of your expectation

THE BIGOT'S FUNERAL (1)

The trip up from Houston sours our stomachs
with each mile: piney woods so dense

men can hide in them for years. State roads
marked with green signs the size of hopelessness.

The last liquor store before the Angelina County line,
a hitchhiker carrying a chainsaw, working damage

from the last hurricane. He won't get beer money
from FEMA anytime soon. Lunch at Lufkin BBQ,

where the black cook still won't meet
the white waitress' eyes over the pass-through,

even though they kissed when they were kids
under the bleachers at the football stadium.

The restaurant's owned by Pentecostals. Each spring
they bless the wooden tables and cast out the demons

who've gathered around fried biscuits, honey
smeared on the vinyl seat backs, the crispy fat

from baby back ribs like anointing oil. Everyone here
is full of sin and judgment. East Texas does that

to you. Makes you think the world's the whole
of the ring from Tyler to Nac to Winnie, makes you

believe in the salvation of a logging truck hurtling
toward you on a one-lane road. We ease back into

the drawl we learned at our mother's breast, ask
for sweet tea and don't say nothing that would shame her.

THE BIGOT'S FUNERAL (2)

The first sign we're really in a Coen brothers' movie
is when the GPS can't find the cemetery.

Been in the family since Texas was a nation,
Uncle Loyce said at the visitation the night before

and we assured Mama *we'll find it.* Turn right
after the old stone house and at the third oak

there's a dirt road. *Yes. We'll be there,* we sighed
and slipped each other a look to say

If we can navigate Amsterdam higher than the three wise men,
we can find the Fenton family plot with a map

and a GPS. But like I said. There are places in the soul
that shouldn't ever be charted and this clearing

in the piney woods is one of them. So we write out
Fenton for the Pakistani woman running the gas station

and grab a handful of those tiny pecan pies because
the baby Jesus only knows what's for lunch

after the service, and she points vaguely back
the way we've come, and we finally jerk the rental

Camry at a hand-painted sign that says *Fenton*
and make it minutes before the minister first intones

Brother Leo loved going to church more than anything.
Which he punctuates with a flourish by punching

play on the pink boom box he's wedged on top
of our Great-Grandmother Maudie's tombstone.

Our chair legs sink into the red clay mud
and just as Mama glares at us over her glasses,

a centipede crawls through the peep-toe
of my left patent pump and lets loose a sting

like the Lord himself is calling me home. Brother Earl
looks at us and knows the sin in our hearts

and the giggles in our throats and tells the gathered
Fentons, Sandlins, and Deckers that *we'll all pray*

now for those here who haven't felt the hand of our Savior.
Brother Leo would want us to on this fine, joyous day.

And it is a fine, joyous day as our waxy, racist
grandfather earns his heavenly rewards

and joins his Father in a better place than this
muddy clearing. And Cousin Donna thinks my shoulders

are shaking from grief so she grips them tight
and kisses my temple, whispers in my ear that there's

pimento cheese sandwiches and deviled eggs
for lunch. And that's the second sign.

CONSPIRACY THEORY

CONTINGENCY PLAN,
AQUARIUM OF THE AMERICAS,
NEW ORLEANS, 2005

The lure of the piranha
to endless streams of school
children: rows of alien

teeth, jaws like prizefighters,
a mob that moves as one
and generates blank fear

in the hearts of river men.
It's the highlight of the tour,
and in the days before the storm

charts showed the spread,
the invasion of black ink
swimming up the Mississippi,

docks stricken in Greenville
and Hannibal, the death
of the Great Lakes in power-point

time lapse. The Assistant Director
sees where this is going.
A great migration, masses

Of thugs flooding over
the levees. Let's call it what
it is. But he clicks his pen,

accepts complicity in extinction.
We do what we must.
The native species. The risk.

Efficiency and euthanasia.
In the flickering fluorescent
hallway behind the tanks he

follows the plan. The city holds
its tropical breath, a ferocious
pause before hell unhinges its jaw.

MY SISTER LOOTS A WINN-DIXIE
AFTER KATRINA

Tonight, Keith Olbermann shows
my sister's face to the world.
I've known her thirty-five years,

but this is a new one:
armfuls of Diet Pepsi and granola bars,
Tylenol in her pocket, a pirate hat

she found in the French Quarter
jaunty on her head. She says
call me Sparrow, does her best

Johnny Depp sneer. Around her people
wheel carry-ons through the aisles,
like it was an airport ankle-deep

in melting ice cream. The camera
shows that a two-gallon water jug
fits perfectly under a dozen diapers

and some Gatorade, and Keith
doesn't understand why people
would steal *luggage*

at a time like this. He wouldn't
last a minute. He'd go for the real
Burberry or Louis Vuitton,

ignoring the cheap Chinese knock-offs
which, let's face it, will roll better
through the smear of shit

outside the Convention Center,
and are less likely to get you mugged.
And my sister is nothing if not

a smart shopper. The camera cuts
to a confused reporter. White and black
faces blur together. Somewhere

a producer struggles to find the thread
of a story and she disappears into
the melee of North Carolton Street.

ODE TO RAY NAGIN AND HIS
CLEAN-SHAVEN SCALP

I have to say you pulled it off—
hiding on the 27th floor of the Hyatt
phoning in the press conferences

to the radio station
you knew they were coming for you
those brothers from Hollygrove

those sisters who didn't vote for you
those aunties who struggled to breathe
in the liquid toxic air

of the Convention Center
and you cussed to beat the band
told America you were *pissed*

you channeled Dr. King you hollered
what we were all screaming in our homes
and I say bless you Ray—you convinced me

you gave a shit
but two years later we learn of the shower
you took on Air Force One

before your meeting with the man
before getting in Blanco's face
and telling the world you made it *work*

it was over an hour before the Secret Service
pounded on the door to say
it was time and everyone was shocked

at how much hot water
snaked through the plane's pipes
and how your scalp shone

when you finally emerged and sat
with your back to the windows of the plane
with your back to the grandfathers

in the full sun on I-10—
their feet gangrenous
and to the kids pushing shopping carts

the busses lined up with no drivers
and to the Dome of the Shelter of Last Refuge
with its skin ripped away—its heart exposed

GREENVILLE, MISSISSIPPI, 1927
after John Barry's Rising Tide

the thing that cracks the soul:
a national guardsman kept brothers apart
at the point of his rifle
(one a refugee on the levee
the other swimming to a roof)

and who's to say he wasn't just scared
not of looters
but of the exodus to Chicago and Detroit
that would follow the flood
the fury of the plantation owners
state senators and governors

so they kept thousands of sharecroppers
trapped on the levees waiting
for the water to go back
to where it came from
hoping the cotton would dry out

they turned away the steamers and barges
let only white women and children board
and April is so much colder than August

from the roofs in town children recognized
the bloated cows of neighbors, called
and responded to uncles in boats
and counted them off like a blues rhythm
Mr Watson's cow
Mr Jefferson's cow
punctured the bodies and
lit them on fire out of boredom

they were on their way
to the levees they were all
on their way to the levees to share space
with surviving livestock and to live like
livestock so the town of Greenville could pay
the salaries of the guardsmen
keeping people on the levees like cattle

and when the Red Cross food came
guess who went to the front of the line

almost eighty years later down river
in New Orleans busses waiting empty
just outside the levee breaks
high on I-10 intersections
the drivers inside telling CNN
i'm not going in there
i promised my wife

and the guardsmen my sister begged
for help were nowhere at night
they disappeared from the flood waters
to the high dry levees of hotel rooms

ST. MARY'S ORPHANAGE: GALVESTON ISLAND
SEPTEMBER 8, 1900

Fear we not, tho' storm clouds round us gather . . .
God of the sea and of the tempest wild.

When the men found them days later
mostly-buried beneath overturned dunes,
they followed one tiny body to another
to whichever Sister had tied them to her.

That first man was probably sunburned
and soaked with the whiskey
he'd been given to numb the stench.
His job: to find bodies, stack and fuel

the beach pyres, so high the smoke
could be seen from Houston. He might
have tripped on a leg or seen the outline
of a small, curled hand, perhaps thought *oh god,*

one more, and gently dug around it. Or
perhaps he was beyond gentleness, beyond
care or counting, and yanked the clothesline
so hard sand shivered along its length

like rosin powder from a violin bow.
Maybe he retched. We know he called
the others, who climbed over the thin ribs
of the dormitory and the rotting fish,

shooed the late summer flies to find him
pulling in the heavy air. We know
what they uncovered: ten women
with ninety children tied to their waists

like chains of Victorian paper dolls,
and found three boys alive in the remains
of a tree to bear witness to the storm.
When the drunk, ravaged men

cleaned the sand from the boys'
mouths, they told of the ocean rising
to fill the Sisters of Charity of the
Incarnate Word like

the Holy Spirit and of the singing,
the hymns, the children's voices that kept
the East Texas pine boards strong
until they weren't anymore.

MOTTO

A suitcase locked and under the bed
        a compass
a list of edible plants
           antibiotics and an optimistic
                pawn-shop pistol.

Today we expect an imminent
        eruption in Alaska
goggles and masks flying
           off the Walmart shelves
                water shipped in on flatbeds.

Cold War warning sirens
        tested and powered.
When the dog's voice becomes
        strange, when the TV sparks
           with static and the anchor's face

blurs as she gives instructions:
        run outside to watch
the instant weather,
        your mouth opening
           to the sky like a lotus.

You've waited for this
        so patiently, packed the trunk
with canned fish, charted routes
        filled the tank with petrol
           while others laughed kindly

at your lists, while they ignored
        the signs and forgot where they left
their keys, while they unlearned what they once
        understood. Pity them their futures,
           their hip-flasks of confidence.

ON THE DEDICATION OF THE SVALBARD GLOBAL SEED VAULT
February 26, 2008

In Norway the sons of Vikings in orange hard hats
sing folk songs behind an ice sculpture—
a polar bear defying extinction—and seventy thousand

varieties of rice rumble by in carts—the very potatoes
Incan kings feasted on—a cowpea collection in jars
three deep—enough to feed the African continent—

and didn't we all press flowers as children—the columbine
your mother said was a sin to pluck—the stigmata
in the passionflower vine—didn't you blow out

dandelion seeds like birthday candles—measure
the weight of pinto beans in your palm as you sifted
out the Texas dirt—weave Indian corn into wreaths

and plant tomatoes in Styrofoam cups—you imagined
climbing all the silos pointing their missile noses
at heaven—and the chessboard wheat fields and fractal

rice paddies seen from an airplane—their patterns broke
your small heart—you finally understood the cans
of peaches hiding in your grandmother's cupboard—

they were on sale—there might be an event—a shift
in the political reality or the weather or a disruption
of some global kind—and it made sense to save

something—although choosing this over that
stopped you cold—you couldn't possibly—who could
possibly choose what to put in a plastic tub in the garage

or a bomb shelter outside Salt Lake—but someone had to
do something crazy—decide to take it all in and screw
the expense—to catalogue it all as a prayer against rising seas

and—shall we call it retribution—so you gratefully cede
the selection of what endures to the tundra—a concrete
Frigidaire for the planet—the steel-hulled audacity of an ark—

CONFESSION

Where the highway ends
the land dissolves into the Gulf—
live oak and mesquite twist

achingly seaward. Alligators
notice her arrival at the house
she remembered the color

of Texas cantaloupe—now
gray. They sun themselves while
the house on pylons casts

the only shade for miles.
A sand dune laps at the edge
of the driveway—morning glory

vines give it traction like guilt.
This is where she learned
a lesson. Something like fear

but not—a premonition
that became a tattoo—
a compass spinning before

a storm. There's no space
inside her now not lit up in
this heat—it's why she came—

to confess to the gulls circling
like something darker—throwing
their bat shadows at her feet.

NEW DEVELOPMENTS AT TEN

At nine-fifty, a fever at the base
of my skull, I chew my thumb's cuticle.

This might be when it happens. They're testing
in our town, they're coughing in the alley

behind my fence. Mumbling men in oily
sweaters feel it first: canaries in the

soup kitchen, the righteous ladlers wearing
sky-blue paper masks to serve them. Who is

to say if I should feel shame, if I could
have released something from a vial by a

school? Would it reflect light into the old
stories in my face? The mother on a

ventilator where she's always belonged,
the poet telling her sister, *stay off*

the subway, stock up on water. Who's to
say I wasn't born to do this? They tease

with the weather first, and I listen for
wind speeds, the perfect storm of a low-

pressure trough, some hidden teleprompter
message that it's okay. We're all okay.

APOCALYPSE
for Scot, after Mellencamp

the man I loved ten years ago
is drinking himself to death
in this season of storms crashing

into Texas—Lake Travis rushing
down cedar-covered hills. he sends
emails to people who once mattered,

one of the twelve steps he takes
even as he pours expensive tequila
into chipped china cups. he sees

my face in the bars on 6th,
in his coffee at Ruta Maya, his
catastrophe-filled dreams of sting rays

gasping for air in roadside ditches.
he'd buy me a mansion if he could,
in Mexico where we'd lie naked

in ant-snaked sand. he cries
god won't leave me alone, baby,
swears *life is temptation*

and the signs are all around:
a dog on three legs, a hand-lettered
sign at the *mercado,* a pitcher

of warm Shiner Bock. he says
it's not the living that'll kill you,
lover. it's the liver.

THE ALMOST
Rothko/Stevens/Hemingway

Standing in front of a black painting
you almost say what you mean, almost
reach out to touch, almost set off the alarm
and the large German guard almost yells
at you, her face almost the color of low winter
sun through branches. But you don't. You can
see that it is meant to make sense.
This is almost order, almost history, but
you can't quite make of it the sense it wants
and it feels like black failure, like liquorice hard
in the pit of your belly. To see the lines bisecting
the black. To have a feeling of black that is
lit from the side, but to only almost say what
it tastes like, to say instead: *disappointment.*

CONSPIRACY THEORY

Say you're right,
and the HAARP antennae array

in Gakona, Alaska has caused every major
hurricane in the last few decades.

High-frequency radio waves exciting
the ionosphere, the fluxgate magnetometer

measuring the results:
a cosmic electric blanket around the earth.

I'll give you that, the polite
acquiescence of metaphor, the wink

that fades to denial under the bald bulb
of an interrogation room.

But through the white noise
of information and half-truths,

fictions, histories and predictions
of hundred-year floods the canary's voice

cuts like a siren. Remember your
sister's cunning, the first time you cheated

at cards, the way you could influence the results
of a high school science experiment.

A politician's lie, a lover's betrayal. The truth
excites the senses. Someone's at the controls.

YOU MUST LEAVE NOW
after Dylan

When I ask what would you pack
if we had thirty minutes to leave
I mean the news of Arizona fires
is rapping at our door. Lately I feel
as brittle as paper—I may start
writing lists on my own arms.
The cats. You. Shoes. An old sheet.

Today the believers pass out sandwiches
and Cokes as if it'll help. God offers
a free lunch like a hit of helium
before a bad punchline. And the
vagabond feeding pigeons says
something to me as I pass. I can't
tell you what he said. I sleep badly

in the glow of the alley's streetlamp,
listen for helicopters and sirens.
The cat tests positive for a retrovirus
and then is cured. I start the kitchen
timer again. My pencils keep
disappearing. *It's hard,* I tell you,
to see these as coincidence.

THIS IS NOT A TEST

The horizon trembles,
shoulders its own heavy heart.

We can only offer you provisions
and wish the bag was lighter,

but we cede hope
to the necessity of weight.

This is the expectation
you've felt since you were six

when the shrimp boats left Port A.
for good under a late July sky.

We have issued the instructions
you require over the short-wave

in the garage. Hurry—flight
is easiest when the pressure

vacuum lifts enough that you
can slip out the back door.

If this had been a test the air
would be alive with sirens

and intent, the whooping cranes
startled but resolute,

the promise of anything
redolent with oleander.

ACKNOWLEDGEMENTS

Thanks to the following journals and magazines for first publishing some of the poems in this collection:

Crab Orchard Review: "St. Mary's Orphanage: Galveston Island September 8, 1900", "The Bigot's Funeral (1)", and "Contingency Plan, Aquarium of the Americas, New Orleans, 2005"

Ecotone: "Sandpipers"

Faultline: "Echo Point, Blue Mountains"

Fruita Pulp: "After the Rain, the Earth Smells Like a Mouth", "Mother My Worry Stone", and "Childhood and Its Rattlesnakes"

Funghi Magazine: "Foray"

Poetry Daily: "First Kiss, Portuguese Man O'War" (reprint)

Puerto del Sol: "Hangi Feast: Rotorua, New Zealand"

Quarterly West: "Bone Collector"

Spoon River Poetry Review: "Wintering at Mooltunya"

Third Coast: "First Kiss, Portuguese Man o'War"

Victory Park: "After Seeing Anne Sexton's Checkbook in a Museum", and "My Parents' Old Acting Troupe, the Alpha Omega Players, Comes to Town"

Thank you to the Department of Languages, Literature, and Mass Communication at Colorado Mesa University and the Faculty Professional Development Fund for support to attend the Bread Loaf Sicily Workshop and other conferences over the years.

And to the many friends and teachers over the years who helped me find my way into poetry through encouragement, community, and thoughtful criticism: Rick Agran, Ai, David Brainard, Kiersten Bridger, Laura Bucko, Scot Casey, Carol Christ, Frank Coons, Doug Cox, Mark Cox, Sandra Dorr, Mark Doty, Douglas Fasching, Monique S. Ferrell, Todd Fuller, Art Goodtimes, Britton Gildersleeve, Kyle Harvey, Jane Hirschfield, Labecca Jones, Linda Leavell, Lisa Lewis, Luis Lopez, Caole Lowry, Tom Lux, Maureen McCarney, Charles McLeod, the Mesa County Public Library Poetry Night group, Juan Morales, John Nizalowski, Uche Ogbuji, Catherine Owens, Robert Payne, Todd Petersen, Randy Phillis, Mindy Rice, David Rivard and our Bread Loaf Sicily Workshop, Danny Rosen, David Rothman, Joe Schell, Tony Spicer, David St. John, Mike Theune, Rosemerry Wahtola Trommer, Laurel Twitchell, Wendy Videlock, Bill Wright, and my amazing husband, TJ Gerlach.

Jennifer Rane Hancock's poems have appeared in several journals, including the *Antioch Review, Spoon River Poetry Review, Crab Orchard Review,* and *Puerto del Sol.* She was nominated for a Pushcart Prize by the editors of *Third Coast,* and was a finalist for the Wabash Prize from the *Sycamore Review.* She lives in Grand Junction, Colorado, where she serves on the city's Commission on Arts and Culture and leads a monthly poetry group at the Mesa County Public Library. Jennifer teaches writing and literature at Colorado Mesa University.